"This is a horribly good way to show that learning about our world can be fun. And seriously important."

Michael Palin

PERILOUS POLES

ANITA GANERI

ILLUSTRATED BY MIKE PHILLIPS

SCHOLASTIC

Scholastic Children's Books,
Euston House, 24 Eversholt Street,
London, NW1 1DB, UK

A division of Scholastic Ltd
London ~ New York ~ Toronto ~ Sydney ~ Auckland
Mexico City ~ New Delhi ~ Hong Kong

Editorial Director: Lisa Edwards
Senior Editor: Jill Sawyer

First published in the UK by Scholastic Ltd, 2010

Text copyright © Anita Ganeri, 2010
Illustrations copyright © Mike Phillips, 2010
Colour by Tom Connell
All rights reserved

ISBN 978 1407 10883 4

Printed and bound by Tien Wah Press Pte. Ltd, Malaysia

2 4 6 8 10 9 7 5 3 1

Contents

INTRODUCTION

Looking for adventure? Fancy heading somewhere really cool? What about a n-ice long trip to the perilous Poles? You'll find them at the freezing-cold ends of the Earth, and you can't get much further away than that. What's that? You're worried you're the sort of person who breaks out in goose pimples if you so much as open the fridge? DON'T PANIC! This horribly useful handbook contains everything you need to survive at the Poles without freezing to death first. Reckon you're ready to break the ice?

So, read on to find out…
• how to pick which perilous Pole to visit
• how to cross a glacier (without falling down a crevasse)
• what *not* to do if you bump into a polar bear
• how to have a pee without getting frostbite
• why a penguin's feet don't freeze on the ice

And that's not all. This handy book is packed with bone-chilling true stories about people who braved the perishing Poles and ended up skating on thin ice. Not to mention life-saving survival tips from real-life polar explorers who found the teeth-chatteringly cold temperatures rather bracing, in fact.

But be warned. The perilous Poles are among the world's wildest places. Even getting there's going to be horribly hard. And despite having loads of new-fangled kit, intrepid polar explorers still run the risk of frostbitten fingers or ending up as a polar bear's lunch. And that's just the tip of the iceberg. So, you'll need to be tough if you're planning on coming back from your polar expedition in one piece. But, despite all the dangers, chances are you'll soon be well and truly bitten by the perishing polar bug. Still keen to pay the perilous Poles a visit? It's time to set off before you get seriously cold feet.

PERILOUS POLES

Exploring is a risky business, especially when the places you're planning to visit are the parkiest on the whole of Planet Earth. The sort of places where it's so colossally cold, the snot will freeze solid inside your nose. It's like walking into a gigantic deep freezer, only, way, way colder than that. Luckily for you, you won't be able to complain because your teeth will be chattering too much. So, where on Earth are the perilous Poles and why on Earth would anyone want to go there in the first place? Keep reading to find out the answers to these chilling questions. This chapter's packed with ice-breaking information to help you feel right at home.

PERILOUS POLES FACT FILE

Name: THE NORTH POLE

What it is: IT'S THE NORTHERNMOST POINT ON EARTH, AT THE NORTHERN END OF THE EARTH'S AXIS (THAT'S AN IMAGINARY LINE RUNNING DOWN THE EARTH'S MIDDLE).

Where is it: IT'S IN THE MIDDLE OF THE FROZEN ARCTIC OCEAN. THE OCEAN AND THE NORTHERNMOST BITS OF THE COUNTRIES AROUND IT (CANADA, USA, GREENLAND, NORWAY AND RUSSIA) ARE CALLED THE ARCTIC.

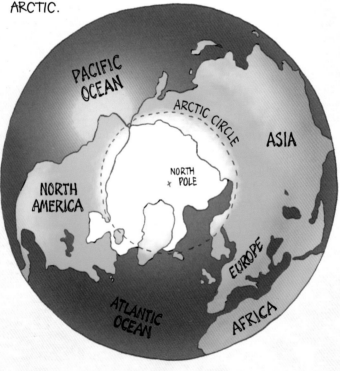

Perilous polar facts:

• The name 'Arctic' comes from the Greek word 'arktos' which means 'bear'. But this isn't a polar bear. It's the bear-shaped pattern of stars twinkling in the northern skies.

• Some horrible geographers count the Arctic as the region inside the (imaginary) Arctic Circle. It's where you get at least one day a year when the sun doesn't set and one day when it doesn't rise.

• The awesome Arctic Ocean's the world's smallest ocean at a paltry 14,000,000 square kilometres or so. It's also the chilliest, covered in ice up to 4 metres thick. Half the ocean's frozen all year round. Other parts melt in spring and freeze again in winter.

• The first person to reach the North Pole was US explorer, Robert Peary, in April 1909. Or was he? His bitter rival, Frederick Cook, claimed to have beaten him to it and accused him of cheating.

THE NORTH POLE: A VISITOR'S GUIDE

• *Getting there:*
There aren't many roads in the Arctic so the best way to arrive is by plane. Then you can set off for the North Pole by dog sled, skidoo, snowmobile or on skis, dragging a sled behind you. Alternatively, hitch a lift in an icebreaker (a steel ship that's specially strengthened for smashing through the ice) or on a super strong sub, travelling under the ice.

• *What to take:*
You can't just nip to the shops at the North Pole, so you'll have to take everything with you. That means warm clothes, shelter, sleeping bag, food – you get the picture. Trouble is, you'll also want to travel light so you don't have to lug too much stuff around. See page 40 for a detailed packing list.

• *When to go:*
Pick the summer for your trip – June, July and August are best. Then you'll have months when the sun never sets, giving you plenty of time for sightseeing. The worst time to go is winter, especially from November to March. Then it's dark for months on end.

• *Where to stay:*
Around the Arctic Circle, there are plenty of villages and towns. But on the way to the Pole itself, you'll have to take your own shelter along. Tents are easiest, but make sure yours is tough enough to stay put in a blizzard, and easy to put up and take down. Or you could build a traditional Inuit igloo. See page 54 for more top tips.

• *Other places to visit:*
Greenland: It's the world's biggest island and about two thirds of it's covered in a 3-kilometre-thick sheet of ice. Head for Disko Bay on the west coast to see the gigantic icebergs clogging up the sea. Some of these whoppers weigh up to 7 million tonnes.
Churchill, Canada: The little town of Churchill in northern Canada has a big claim to fame. It lies right on a polar bear migration route and in September and October these cool creatures can often be seen wandering towards the coast. The safest way to watch them is on an organized tour but DO NOT GET OUT OF THE BUS!

Across the top of the world

Svalbard, Arctic Norway, 29 May 1969

On 29 May 1969, British explorer, Wally Herbert (1934–2007) and his team, reached a small, rocky island in Svalbard, and made history. The four men had completed the first surface crossing of the Arctic Ocean, a perilous journey of 6,080 kilometres that had taken 15 months. A journey no one thought was even possible.

WALLY HERBERT

As a boy, Wally dreamed of exploring the world but his dad made him join the army instead. Then he had an amazing stroke of luck. He was sitting on a bus when a newspaper dropped from the luggage rack into his lap, and fell open at the jobs' page. One of the ads caught Wally's eye – team members wanted for an expedition to Antarctica. It was Wally's perfect job. He spent many years in Antarctica, mapping vast areas of unexplored land and learning to drive a dog sled. Then he turned his attention north. Soon he was planning his greatest expedition yet – crossing the icy wastes of the Arctic Ocean by foot. No one had ever tried this before. The shifting pack ice made it just too treacherous.

Wally and his three-man team set off from Point Barrow in Alaska on 21 February 1968, with a team of 40 dogs. They needed to complete the crossing before the ice melted. But it was going to be horribly tough. Beneath their feet, the ice constantly broke apart and crashed together again. At any time, they, and their dogs, could be swallowed up. By July, they had covered more than 1,000 kilometres and they decided to set up camp.

For months, they shivered in bone-numbing temperatures of -50 C and suffered days of pitch darkness as they drifted around the Pole. At one point, they had to move their campsite when the ice beneath them began to crack up.

The following year, they continued their journey and reached the North Pole on 6 April 1969. It was an astonishing achievement. But their ordeal wasn't over. They still had a very long way to go to complete their epic crossing. Two weeks after reaching Svalbard, the men and dogs were picked up by helicopter, safe and well. Their remarkable feat was later described as being 'among the greatest triumphs of human skill and endurance', and has never been repeated…

PERILOUS POLES FACT FILE

Name: THE SOUTH POLE

What is it: IT'S THE SOUTHERNMOST POINT ON EARTH, AT THE SOUTHERN END OF THE EARTH'S AXIS (REMEMBER THAT?).

Where is it: IT'S IN ANTARCTICA, A COLOSSAL CONTINENT COVERED IN ICE. IT SITS IN THE MIDDLE OF A VAST, WINDSWEPT PLAIN ON TOP OF ICE RECKONED TO BE AROUND 2.7 KILOMETRES THICK. NEARBY, THERE'S A RED–AND–WHITE STRIPED POLE, TOPPED WITH A METAL BALL. IT'S NOT THE REAL THING BUT IT'LL LOOK GOOD IN YOUR HOLIDAY SNAPS.

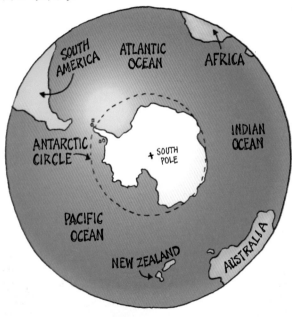

Perilous polar facts:

• The name 'Antarctica' comes from the Greek meaning 'opposite the bear'. It's the world's fifth largest continent, covering about 14 million square kilometres (that's almost one and half times the size of the USA).

• About 98 per cent of Antarctica is covered by ice up to

HEADS IT EXISTS, TAILS IT DOESN'T!

5 kilometres thick, making it the largest ice cube on Earth. Buried beneath this enormous ice sheet are vile volcanoes and massive mountains.

• Awesome Antarctica is surrounded by the Southern Ocean. It's well known to suffering sailors as the stormiest ocean on Earth. In winter, large stretches of sea freeze over, doubling Antarctica's size.

• The Greeks who named Antarctica guessed it existed but nobody actually saw it until 1820. The first person to reach the South Pole was Norwegian explorer Roald Amundsen in December 1911.

EARTH—SHATTERING FACT

Antarctica was once toasty warm, and nestled near the Equator. It's true! Instead of ice, it was covered in tropical forests where dinosaurs and other prehistoric reptiles roamed. So how on Earth did it get to be so cold? Well, 200 million years ago, it was part of a 'super-continent' with Australia and South America. Ever so slowly, they split apart and became separated by sea. Antarctica drifted further and further south and got nippier and nippier...

THE SOUTH POLE: A VISITOR'S GUIDE

• *Getting there*:

Antarctica's the most isolated place on Earth so getting there's no picnic. Hitch a lift on a plane or a ship but be prepared for long delays if the weather turns nasty. Then continue your journey by ski or snowmobile. You'll have to pull your own sled. Dogs have been banned from Antarctica since 1994 because it was feared they'd spread deadly diseases to the local seals.

• *What to take*:

Much the same as for the North Pole (see pages 12 and 40). If you're a scientist, everything you need will be brought by ship or plane. And all your rubbish will be shipped home again in case it harms Antarctica's fragile environment.

• *When to go*:

As with the North Pole, summer's the best time to go. But bear in mind, the seasons are reversed in the southern hemisphere so December, January and February are summer there.

• *Where to stay*:

Fond of camping? You'll need to be. You'll be spending a lot of your time in a tent. Remember to mark your campsite with a marker or flag, in case a blizzard blows up and smothers it in snow while you're out and about. Scientists should head for their nearest research station.

• *Other places to visit*:

Mount Erebus: It's the planet's most southerly volcano, towering 3,794 metres above Ross Island in the Ross Sea. It was first climbed in 1908 but take care, if you're planning on pootling up. This beauty's still active and only specially trained scientists are allowed up.

Lake Vostok: It's one of around 145 lakes in Antarctica, but it's buried under FOUR KILOMETRES of ice so it's horribly hard to reach. Scientists spotted it with ice-penetrating radar and reckon it's the size of Lake Ontario, one of the world's largest lakes. They're now trying to find out if there's anything lurking in this long-lost lake.

EARTH-SHATTERING FACT

Less than half a per cent of Antarctica is ice-free. The tops of massive mountains poke up through the ice, including Mount Vinson (4,900 metres), the highest point on the continent. To reach the top of this freaky peak, you'll need to be an expert climber and skier, not to mention coping with biting cold and gale-force winds, and lugging a backbreaking load. But the breathtaking views from the top should be the icing on the cake.

If you've slogged all the way to the North or South Poles, you don't want to end up in the wrong place. There are six possible Poles to pick from.

North...

1 Geographic North Pole: it's the point at the northern end of the Earth's axis, located about 700 km north of Greenland in the middle of the Arctic Ocean. If you're standing at this perilous Pole, everything points south.

2 Magnetic North Pole: it's the place you'll pitch up in if you follow your compass and head 'north'. But, be careful, this puzzling pole changes position from day to day. It's currently located off the coast of northern Canada but it has shifted hundreds of kilometres since it was first tracked down in 1831.

3 Northern Pole of Inaccessibility: it's the spot on the Arctic Ocean that's furthest from land. Your nearest neighbours are about 1,000 kilometres away so you can't just drop round for a cup of tea.

...and South

4 Geographic South Pole: it's the point at the southern end of the Earth's axis on the continent of Antarctica. If you're standing at this perilous Pole, everything points north. But, because the ice at the Pole keeps shifting, the Pole marker has to be moved by about 10 metres a year.

5 Magnetic South Pole: it's the place you pitch up in if you follow your compass and head 'south'. Like the nifty North Pole, it's constantly moving and you'll have to make for the coast of Wilks Land in Antarctica to track it down today.

6 The Southern Pole of Inaccessibility: it's the point on Antarctica that's the furthest from any coast. If you find yourself stranded here, you're in for a horribly long journey home.

Name that ... perilous polar feature

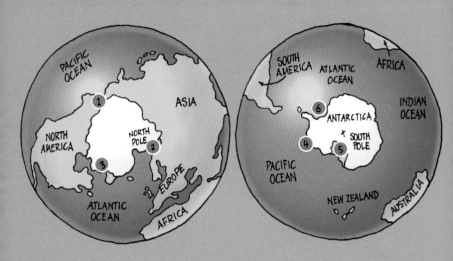

Arctic...

1 Name: **Bering Strait**

Description: A narrow sea passage between Siberia and Alaska.

Named after: Vitus Bering (1680–1741). Brave Bering was sent by Russian Tsar Peter the Great to map the frozen wastes of Siberia and prove that Asia and North America were divided by sea. He crossed the strait in 1728 but sadly died on a second expedition, when he was stranded by ice on Bering Island, named after, well, er, him.

VITUS BERING

WILLIAM BARENTS

2 Name: **Barents Sea**
Description: Part of the Arctic Ocean, to the north of Norway and Russia.
Named after: William Barents (c 1550–1597). Daring Barents set sail several times to search for the Northeast Passage – a new sea route across the far north of Russia. His third voyage ended in disaster when his ship got stuck in the ice and he was forced to spend a freezing winter in the Arctic. He survived the awful ordeal only to perish on the way home.

3 Name: **Frobisher Bay**
Description: A large bay off Baffin Island in northern Canada.
Named after: Martin Frobisher (c 1535–94). Feisty Frobisher was the first explorer from Europe to see the bay which he wrongly thought was the start of the Northwest Passage – a sea route across the far north of North America. He also collected a load of old rocks he wrongly reckoned were full of precious gold.

MARTIN FROBISHER

THADDEUS BELLINGSHAUSEN

Antarctica…
4 Name: **Bellingshausen Sea**
Description: Part of the Southern Ocean, on the western side of the Antarctic Peninsula.
Named after: Thaddeus Bellingshausen (1778–1852). In 1820, ice-breaking Bellingshausen crossed the Antarctic Circle and became the first person to see Antarctica. Trouble was, he didn't take

much notice and simply carried on sailing. He was probably too busy heating up cannonballs for his shipboard sauna to be bothered with new-fangled things like that.

5 Name: **Ross Ice Shelf**
Description: The largest ice shelf in Antarctica, about the size of France.
Named after: James Clark Ross (1800–62). Dashing Ross was the first to see the colossal ice shelf in January 1841 when its great bulk blocked his ships' path. Not that that spoiled Ross's fun. On a second trip, he moored next to the ice and held a fancy dress party on an enormous floe. Originally called simply

JAMES CLARK ROSS

'the Barrier', it was later rather catchily renamed.

JAMES WEDDELL

6 Name: **Weddell Sea**
Description: Part of the Southern Ocean, off the east coast of the Antarctic Peninsula.
Named after: James Weddell (1787–1834). Globetrotting Weddell had already given his name to a type of seal when he sailed into this sea in 1823. Oddly, he wrote in his diary that there was 'not a particle of ice of any description was to be seen'. Odd because this particular patch of polar water is usually choked up with horribly thick pack ice.

IN THE FREEZER

You'll need to brace yourself for some seriously hostile conditions at the Poles. And we're not talking about a slight nip in the air. Or a festive flurry of snow. The Poles are the coldest, windiest and iciest places on Earth, and you don't get much wilder than that. One false step and you'll freeze to death. Then there's the scenery – nothing but ice for miles and miles. Never mind, if you ever stop sh-sh-shivering, you'll soon get over the sh-sh-shock. To let you know what you're in for, here's the latest polar weather report…

Polar weather report

A very frosty welcome to the polar weather service. If you're dreaming of a white Christmas, you've come to the right place. Today, at the North and South Poles, the weather is likely to be…

• *Freezing cold…*
You won't be surprised to hear the perilous Poles are officially the coldest places on Earth. If you're heading for the North Pole in winter, expect teeth-chattering temperatures of around -35°C. Better to wait until summer when it's a toasty 0°C. The South Pole's even colder. Even in the middle of summer, temperatures don't rise above a perishing -25°C and, in winter, can plummet to a bone-chilling -65°C and below. Brrrr.

EARTH-SHATTERING FACT

The Poles are so cold because the Earth's surface is curved. The sun's rays hit the top and bottom at a wide angle, meaning they're weaker and more spread out. To make matters worse, the white colour of the ice reflects most of the sunlight straight back into space. This is called the albedo effect and, put simply, it means light colours reflect heat away and dark colours soak it up.

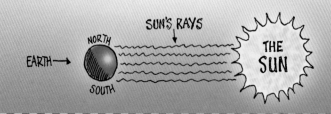

• *Dry as a desert…*
Awesome Antarctica's the largest desert on Earth, beating the scorching Sahara into second place. It's true! But forget sand dunes and palm trees. Antarctica counts as a desert because it gets less than 250 millimetres of rain and snow each year, and most places only get a fifth of that. The Dry Valleys, near McMurdo Sound, really live up to their name. No rain has fallen in these parched parts for at least TWO MILLION YEARS.

• *Blowing a gale…*
And, finally … wind could be a problem today. It's usually blowing a gale. In fact, the Poles are the windiest place on the planet, and we're not talking a gentle breeze. These winds blast along at a howling 200 km/ph or more. Worse still, the stronger the wind's blowing, the colder you're going to feel. So, at -35°C with a 50-km/ph wind, it'll actually feel like -80°C, plenty cold enough to freeze bare flesh.

I NEED TO CHILL OUT!

HORRIBLE HEALTH WARNING

A blizzard's a wild winter storm where howling winds whip the snow along. And the world's worse blizzards blow up in, yep you've guessed it, the Poles. Woe betide you if you get caught up in one, especially as they can strike without warning. The best thing to do is to sit the storm out in the safety of your tent. Don't bother going outside. You won't be able to see the end of your nose, never mind find your way back to camp.

Weird polar weather

Awesome aurorae
They're spectacular displays of bright, flashing lights that appear on clear, cold nights in the polar skies. Prepare to be dazzled. They happen when electrical particles stream from the sun and crash into gases in the Earth's atmosphere. Their technical names are aurora borealis (northern lights) and aurora australis (southern lights).

Stunning solar haloes
They're bright rings that appear around the sun when light's bent by ice crystals in clouds high up in the atmosphere. And they're nothing to do with angels. They're sometimes seen with 'sun dogs' – luminous spots on either side of the sun, and 'fog bows' – like rainbows but missing the pretty colours. They're usually seen in winter.

Incredible ice blink

It's a bright, white glare you see underneath a low cloud. It might mean there's ice ahead but it's too far away for you to see. If the underneath of the cloud's darkish grey, it could be a case of water sky. That means the cloud is over a patch of open water. Both of these freaky phenomena can be useful if you've left your binoculars behind.

Marvellous mirages

Seeing things? It may be a mirage (when light's bent as it passes through layers of air of different temperatures). In 1818, a mirage changed the course of Arctic exploration when British sailor, John Ross, saw a range of mountains blocking his way into Lancaster Sound. Ross named them the Croker Mountains, turned his ship round and headed home. What a shame, especially as the mountains weren't really there. If misty-eyed Ross had carried on, he'd have found the Northwest Passage and claimed the handsome reward.

PERILOUS POLES FACT FILE

Name: ICE SHEET
What it is: A HUGE SHEET OF ICE FORMED FROM SNOW THAT FALLS OVER THOUSANDS OF YEARS.
Where it is: GREENLAND AND ANTARCTICA

Perilous polar facts:
• The Antarctic ice sheet is the biggest slab of ice on Earth. It holds around 30 million cubic kilometres of ice – about 1,000 million million million ice lollies' worth – and it's around 3 million years old.
• More than three-quarters of groovy Greenland is covered by another enormous ice sheet up to 3 kilometres thick. The ice is so bloomin' heavy, the land under it has sunk.
• An ice shelf's a colossal floating chunk of ice stuck to the edge of an ice sheet. And not something you'd put this book on.
• Thousands of gigantic masses of ice, called glaciers, flow from ice sheets. They form when snow falls in layers and the bottom layers get squashed into ice.

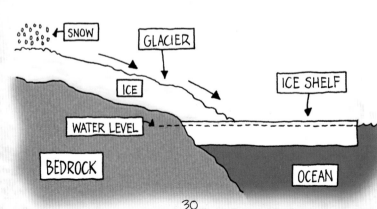

SNOW

GLACIER

ICE SHELF

ICE

WATER LEVEL

BEDROCK

OCEAN

Could you be a glaciologist*?
* That's the posh name for a scientist who studies ice.

Which of these cold, hard facts are true?

1 A baby iceberg's called a growler. True/False

2 The biggest iceberg was the size of a house. True/False

3 Most of an iceberg pokes up above the sea. True/False

4 Icebergs can last for years and years. True/False

5 The biggest glacier's in Greenland. True/False

6 Glaciers 'flow' like rivers. True/ False

7 Glaciers are sparkly white. True/False

8 It's bad luck to laugh at a glacier. True/ False

Answers:

1 TRUE. A baby iceberg breaks off from the end of an ice sheet or glacier. Strangely, glaciologists call this 'calving' but they don't call the baby berg a calf. They call it a growler instead. Talk about confusing. A growler's about the size of a small car so it's only a baby in iceberg terms. In Greenland and Antarctica, thousands of growlers are born every year.

2 FALSE. It was much, much bigger than that – the size of the whole country of Belgium, in fact. The crew of the USS *Glacier* spotted this monster berg in 1956 in Antarctica. Well, they could hardly miss it, could they? A year later, the tallest iceberg ever known was seen in the Arctic. It towered almost 170 metres above the sea, as high as a 55-storey building. Bet you'd get a very n-ice view from the top.

3 FALSE. Only about 10 per cent of an iceberg pokes up out of the sea. The rest lies underwater, making bergs a horrible hazard for ships. To make matters worse, bergs drift about on the ocean currents, so it's tricky to plot their position on a map. Today, ships use new-fangled radar and satellite technology to keep tabs on icebergs. Trouble is, this only works well with bigger bergs. By the time you spot a growler, it might already be too late.

4 TRUE. Most icebergs melt after a year or two, but some can last much longer than that. One ancient berg was reckoned to be a staggering 45 years old. Over the years the bergs can drift thousands of kilometres from their original home. Eventually they reach warmer waters and start to melt.

5 FALSE. To check out the biggest glacier, you'll need to head for the other end of the world. The gigantic Lambert Glacier

in eastern Antarctica's a record-breaking 515 kilometres long and more than 40 kilometres wide. The Beardmore is another giant, measuring more than 160 kilometres. But it's even more famous as the route taken by Captain Scott on his epic 1911–12 trek to the South Pole.

6 TRUE. Well, sort of. Glaciers certainly move downhill, like rivers, pulled down by the force of gravity (gravity is the force that brings things down to the ground). But there's more to it than that. Even though it looks rock solid, the ice inside a glacier is a bit like soft plastic that gets squashed and squeezed by the ice on top, and starts moving. Most glaciers move very slowly, at around 2–3 metres a day, so you could easily outrun one. Hopefully.

7 FALSE. Some glaciers glisten deep blue because of the way sunlight gets broken up as it passes through the ice. Others look horrible grey and grubby because of the tonnes of rock, snow and dirty they drag along. And a few gorgeous glaciers turn a delicate shade of pink because of tiny plants called algae that live in the top layers of the ice.

8 TRUE. At least, the local Inuit people of Greenland think so and they treat glaciers with great respect. They believe if you speak or laugh as you're paddling past a glacier, it'll take offence and dump a load of ice in your boat. Oh well, you have been warned…

Glacier safety guide

1 DO wear crampons. They're sharp spikes that you strap to your climbing boots. Glaciers can be slippery characters and it's dead easy to lose your footing. Try to keep as many spikes in contact with ice as you can and dig them in firmly.

2 DO rope up. Before even setting foot on the glacier, make sure you're tied to the other members of your team with a long rope. That way, if one of you falls in, the others will be able to haul you out.

3 DO carry an ice axe. While you're walking, use it like a walking stick to prod the snow to see if it's firm. If your axe goes straight through, find somewhere else to cross. If you feel yourself falling, you'll need to perform an ice-axe arrest.

Here's what to do…

Ⓐ AS YOU SLIDE, ROLL OVER TO FACE THE ICE, FEET DOWN...

PICK
ADZE
SHAFT
SPIKE

Ⓑ KEEP THE SHARP PICK OF THE AXE FACING AWAY FROM YOU...

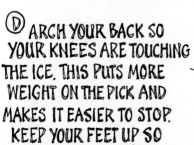

Ⓒ FIRMLY DIG THE PICK INTO THE ICE AND HOLD ON TO THE HANDLE TIGHTLY...

Ⓓ ARCH YOUR BACK SO YOUR KNEES ARE TOUCHING THE ICE. THIS PUTS MORE WEIGHT ON THE PICK AND MAKES IT EASIER TO STOP. KEEP YOUR FEET UP SO YOUR CRAMPONS DON'T SNAG...

PERILOUS POLES FACT FILE

Name: SEA ICE
What is it: IT'S A SPECIAL SALTY TYPE OF ICE FORMED
WHEN SEA WATER FREEZES.
Where is it: ARCTIC OCEAN; SOUTHERN OCEAN

Perilous polar facts:
• The Arctic Ocean's covered in a year-round layer of sea ice a few metres thick. It melts back in spring and summer, then freezes over again in winter.
• In winter, around 20 million square kilometres of the Southern Ocean freezes. This more than doubles the size of Antarctica.
• Pack ice is made of broken bits of sea ice that drift on the wind and waves. Free-floating pieces of pack ice are called floes and can measure more than 10 kilometres across.
• As they drift, cracks appear in the floes or smash into each other to form huge ridges. Making it horribly a easy place for a ship to get trapped in the pack ice.

Sea-ice spotter's guide

Which of these cool customers *isn't* a type of sea ice?

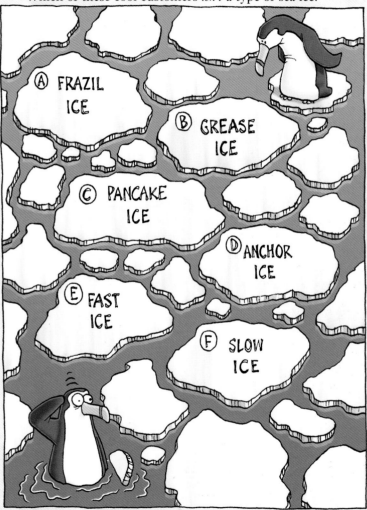

Ⓐ FRAZIL ICE

Ⓑ GREASE ICE

Ⓒ PANCAKE ICE

Ⓓ ANCHOR ICE

Ⓔ FAST ICE

Ⓕ SLOW ICE

Answers:

The odd one out is **f)** but all of the rest are melt-in-the -mouth true!

a) Tiny, needle-shaped crystals of frazil ice form as the sea starts to ice over in winter. Each minuscule crystal is a paltry 3–4 millimetres wide. When enough of them join together, they make a slushy mixture that floats on the sea.

b) As the frazil ice freezes further, it forms a layer of smooth, thin ice that gives the sea an oily sheen. Which is how grease ice gets it greasy name. At first, this grease ice is thin and dark; later it gets thicker and darker.

c) If the sea's rough, the frazil ice freezes into pancake-shaped disks of ice. These pancakes have upturned edges from bashing into each other like d-icey dodgem cars.

d) This ice grows underwater where it's fixed, or anchored, to the sea bed. It's found along the edges of ice shelves in Antarctica and the floating ends of glaciers. But it can also stick itself to rocks, ropes and even unfortunate sea creatures like sponges.

e) This ice has got nothing to do with speed, but got its name because it's stuck fast to the shore or between two icebergs. In fact, it's so firmly fixed in places it can't be budged by the wind or currents.

f) There's no such thing as slow ice.

SURVIVAL TIP

If you're planning on crossing sea ice, look out for clear blue or green patches. They show where the strongest bits of ice are. Usually. Even then, there's no guarantee you won't fall in. Ice that was safe an hour ago could quickly become too weak to take your weight. If you DO fall in, DON'T PANIC. OK, the water's freezing cold and you'll have trouble breathing. But you'll probably have at least 15 minutes before you freeze to death.

PARKY POLAR EXPLORERS

If you're dead set on exploring the Poles, read this chapter before you set off. It could save your life. Polar exploration is horribly exciting but it's also horribly difficult and risky. For a start, frostbite's a serious danger in the freezing conditions so dressing the part is essential. Then, after a hard day's sledging, what could be better than a nice, hot meal and a warm, dry bed. The last thing you'll need is to snuggle down in your sleeping bag only to find it has frozen solid. Yep, you're in for a thrilling ride. But don't worry – you're not alone. To help you plan your expedition and get you back in one piece, this chapter's crammed with vital survival advice from plucky polar explorers who've been there and done that. But first, you need to find out what to put on your polar packing list.

YOU FORGOT YOUR TOOTHBRUSH!

POLAR PACKING LIST
1 CLOTHES

Thermal undies: leggings and long-sleeved vest worn next to your skin.

Thermal socks: with sock liners (you can also wear this layer in bed).

Thin, fleecy top: for extra insulation against the cold.

Trekking trousers: made from moleskin or stretchy, synthetic material.

Windproof jacket: it's windproof and waterproof.

Puffer jacket: extra warm for extra cold days.

Over-trousers: like the jacket, it's also 'breathable' to let sweat escape.

Hat: made from fleece with flaps that cover your ears.

Balaclava: for wearing under your hat if it's very cold.

Face mask: to stop your breath freezing on to your skin.

Gloves: wear a thin, thermal pair with fleece-lined mittens on top.

Goggles: to protect your eyes from the sun's glare.

Boots: specially designed with thick rubber soles for insulation. Make sure you've got room to wiggle your toes.

SURVIVAL TIP

By wearing several layers of clothes, you'll trap warm air next to your skin and let sweat escape. Otherwise, it'll draw the heat away and freeze on to your skin. Then it's a slippery slope to full-blown frostbite and hypothermia (see page 47).

2 SHELTER

Tent: pick a tent that's shaped like a pyramid. It'll be less likely to get blown away. It needs a double 'skin', that's breathable on the outside and insulated on the inside. Build a snow wall around it to protect it from the wind. In the morning, you'll need to scrape the ice from the inside of your tent. That's where your breath froze solid in the night.

Sleeping bag: A down-filled bag is warmest; with a hood you can pull tight around your head. OK, so you'll look like an Egyptian mummy, but at least you won't be long dead. Make sure your bag's a snug fit. If there's too much air around you, you'll feel horribly chilly.

3 GETTING AROUND/STAYING IN TOUCH

Pulk: it's a small sled you drag behind you, carrying everything you need. Pick a pulk made from a strong, lightweight, synthetic material or from fibreglass.

• Skis: it's (usually) quicker to ski across ice than walk but you need to choose the right skis. Modern explorers use skis made from wood covered in super-strong plastic.

• Satellite phone: new-fangled satellite phones let you stay in touch even at the North Pole. Don't forget to pack some spare batteries.

GPS: a handheld GPS (Global Positioning System) will help you plot your position and stay on course. So you won't have to bother with boring maps. It works by picking up information from satellites out in space.

Personal locator beacon: it's a gadget about the size and shape of a mobile phone that sends out a signal if you're lost or in trouble. The signal is transmitted through the international search and rescue satellite system so rescuers know where you are.

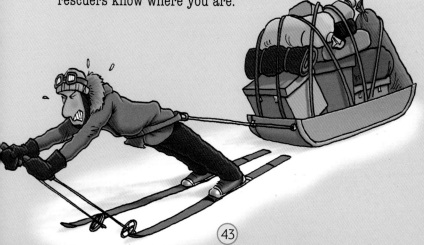

4 FOOD AND COOKING

Stove: a paraffin-fuelled stove, like a camping stove, is best but make sure there's lots of ventilation in your tent.

Food: keeping warm burns up loads of energy and you'll also be lugging a heavy load along. So you'll need to scoff around 3,000 calories a day – that's twice as much as you usually eat. So, what's on today's menu?

Breakfast:

Porridge, muesli, raisins, milk powder (mixed with water), sugar, tea, coffee or hot chocolate

Lunch:

Nuts, sweets, chunks of sausage, cheese, crackers, chocolate, cakes, energy bars

Pack these in a day bag and munch on something every hour or so. You'll have to eat on the move – it's too c-c-cold to stop for lunch.

Dinner:

Freeze-dried meal (such as veggie pasta, curry or stew), mixed with water.

Freeze-dried pudding (such as rice pudding or apple and custard), mixed with water.

Tea, coffee or hot chocolate

SURVIVAL TIP

Keep your day bag close to your body to keep it warm. You'll find yourself spitting teeth if you try to chomp on a deep-frozen choccie bar. If the bar has turned to ice, stick it in your pocket until it's soft enough to take a bite.

Could you be a polar explorer?

Six supercool survival tips

1 Dying for a pee? Be quick if you're popping outside. Otherwise, you run the risk of frostbite and (at the North Pole) prying polar bears. If you need a poo, dig a big hole in the snow and line it with a bin liner. Don't forget to take the bag with you when you leave camp. The poo will have frozen solid by then so it shouldn't have a strong pong.

2 It's dead easy to get dehydrated at the Poles because the air you're breathing's dry as a bone. Drink plenty of water, even if you don't feel like it. Simply shove some snow in a saucepan and melt it over the stove. Then leave it to cool, and slurp. Simple.

3 Never take your gloves off when you go outside. EVER. Within seconds, your fingers will be frozen solid with frostbite. Get used to doing up zips, putting up tents, eating and drinking, with your gloves firmly on.

4 To stop toothpaste and other stuff like shampoo freezing solid, stick tubes and bottles inside your clothes or sleeping bag. Well, it beats snuggling up to a teddy bear.

5 Having a wash at the Poles is snow laughing matter. After all, you can't just nip off for a nice, long bath. The best thing to do is grab a handful of snow and start scrubbing. It might tingle a bit but grit your teeth.

6 At night, get into your tent backwards, take your boots off and bash the snow off them outside. Then you won't drag snow into the tent and end up with a soggy sleeping bag. (Don't leave your boots outside. They'll have frozen solid by morning.)

EARTH—SHATTERING FACT

It helps to be fabulously fit and healthy to survive at the Poles. So you'll need to train hard before you set off. For starters, practise packing and unpacking your sled, putting up and taking down your tent, melting snow for food, navigating with your GPS, and skiing long distances. Finding somewhere nice and cold will help you acclimatize. One plucky explorer trained for her trip to the South Pole by spending hours in a frozen-fish van.

POLAR MEDICAL MANUAL

HYPOTHERMIA

Symptoms: You feel horribly groggy and sluggish. You can't speak or think clearly. Then you start shivering uncontrollably, and your pulse rate and breathing slow down. Eventually, you collapse and lose consciousness. If you don't get warm again quickly, you're quite likely to die.

Cause: A drop in body temperature brought on by extreme cold. Your body temperature's normally around 37°C but even a drop of 2 degrees can be fatal.

Patients' notes:
- Get out of the cold *quickly*.
- Then start warming up *slowly*.
- Get into your sleeping bag to get warm.
- Slurp plenty of hot drinks.

FROSTBITE

Symptoms: Your fingers, feet, ears and nose are most at risk. First, they start tingling and the skin turns waxy white. Then they go numb. Eventually, they go hard and black, and may drop off.

Cause: Parts of your body get so cold, the skin and flesh start to freeze and die.

Patients' notes:
• Thaw out the frozen bits *slowly* but don't rub them.
• Dunk them in warm (not hot) water for an hour or so.
• When the skin's red and swollen, it's warm enough. (Note: this bit will HURT!)
• Pull faces to stop your face getting frostbitten.

SNOW BLINDNESS

Symptoms: Your eyes sting and feel gritty, as if they're full of sand. You don't actually go blind but it's horribly painful to open your eyes.

Cause: The glare of the sun's rays reflected off the ice or snow. It's like having sunburned eyeballs.

Patients' notes:
• Get into a dark place – any light will hurt your eyes.
• Cover your eyes with a damp, cool cloth.
• Don't rub your eyes (however itchy they get).
• Wear goggles or sunglasses to protect your eyes, even on dull days.

SURVIVAL TIP

Teaming up with a 'buddy' could save your life. The idea is you look
out for each other at all times. Apart from making sure you don't
get horribly lost, your buddy will be able to spot the tell-tale signs
of frostbite and hypothermia, even if you can't see them yourself.

Five plucky polar pioneers
Henry Worsley, Britain

In 2008, Henry Worsley and two companions
set off in the footsteps of legendary British
explorer, Ernest Shackleton (1874–1922), to
reach the South Pole. All three were related to
the original members of Shackleton's team.
Sadly, a century before, awful weather had
forced Shackleton back just 180 kilometres
from his goal. This time, Henry was luckier. His team reached
the Pole safely, then hitched a lift on a plane outta there.

Rune Gjeldnes, Norway
Daring Rune had already skied across the
Arctic Ocean and Greenland when he headed
to Antarctica in 2005. It took him 93 days
to ski across the continent, on his own and
without any outside help. He had to lug
everything he needed along with him on
a heavy sled. On the way, he faced freezing cold
conditions, treacherous crevasses and icy winds. Despite this,
he kept horribly cheerful by listening to his favourite tunes.

Hannah McKeand, Britain

Before she set off to ski alone to the North Pole in 2008, plucky Hannah piled on the pounds by guzzling choccie puddings to help her survive the hard slog. She also packed some brand-new battery-powered footwarmers to slip into her ski boots. Sadly, Hannah's epic trek was cut short when she crashed into a crevasse and hurt her back, arm and leg. Luckily, she was able to use her satellite phone to call for help.

Lewis Gordon Pugh, South Africa

In 2005, Lewis smashed the world record for the most southerly ice swim. He dived into the Southern Ocean off Antarctica, dressed only in a pair of swimming trunks and a swimming cap. Lewis spent a bone-chilling 18 minutes and 10 seconds in the freezing cold water. After three minutes, his hands and feet went numb. After six minutes, he couldn't feel his arms and legs. Back home, he trains in a pool filled with half a tonne of ice. Brrrr.

Gustavus McLeod, USA

For years, Gustavus dreamed of flying to the North Pole and, in 2000, he got his chance. But his was no flash, new-fangled plane. Alarmingly, it only had one engine and its cockpit was open to the elements. Over the next 15 hours, Gustavus suffered a frostbitten chin and a bad burn on his stomach from the electric heating coil in his flying suit. Despite this, he managed to reach the North Pole, navigating by the sun when his GPS froze.

PERILOUS POLAR LIVING

You might think you're horribly hardy. The sort of person who doesn't crack, no matter what's thrown at you. Are you sure about that? It's one thing nipping out on a winter's day for a friendly snowball fight, then nipping back indoors again to get nice and warm by the fire. But days of feeling chilled to the bone, blasted by blizzards and bored rigid by the icy views can seriously grind you down. Before long, you'll quite fancy bumping into a polar bear. If you can remember why you came to the perishing Poles in the first place. Luckily for you, some very cool customers already live near the North Pole, despite the horribly hostile conditions. They're called the Inuit, and they've offered to show you the ropes.

PERILOUS POLES FACT FILE

Name: **THE INUIT**
Who are they? **GROUPS OF AROUND 150,000 PEOPLE WHO LIVE IN THE ARCTIC.**
Where do they live? **ALASKA, CANADA, GREENLAND**

Perilous polar facts:
• The Inuit have lived in the Arctic for more than 4,000 years so they know the perilous place like the backs of their hands.
• Traditionally, the Inuit lived as nomads, fishing and hunting animals, such as seals, whales and polar bears for food and materials for making clothes, weapons and tools.
• In the Inuit language, the word 'Inuit' simply means 'the people'. One person is an 'Inuk'. Other Inuit words you might know are 'kayak' and 'anorak'.
• Many polar explorers (remember Wally Herbert?) learned life-saving Inuit survival skills like making clothes and driving a dog sled as part of their polar training.

Five ways to live like the Inuit

1 Knit yourself a qiviut hat. The Inuit are experts at keeping warm and traditionally make their clothes from super-snug animal skin and fur. Caribous and seal are firm favourites but for the warmest hat you'll ever wear, you can't beat qiviut (ki-vee-ute). It's musk ox wool, in case you were wondering. It's grey-brown in colour, and sensationally soft and warm. The only problem is getting it from the musk ox without being speared by their massive horns. Best to wait until the qiviut falls off naturally in spring. Then give it a good wash, spin it into yarn and get knitting. You'll need about 60 grams of qiviut for one hat. (An adult musk ox sheds around 40 hats' worth of wool a year.)

2 Build yourself an igloo. Picture the scene. You're out on a seal-hunting trip, a blizzard's on the horizon and you realize you've forgotten your tent. What on Earth do you do? Easy, peasy. You build yourself an igloo, just like an Inuit hunter would do. You'll need some help, though. Even the expert Inuit need three men for the job – one to cut the blocks of snow, one to build, and one to plug up any gaps. Incredibly, it take them less than an hour to pitch the perfect igloo. It's bound to take you longer (remember to keep your gloves on) but it'll be worth it in the end. It may be blowing a gale outside but, because snow's a brilliant insulator (a material that traps heat), inside your igloo you'll be toasty.

3 Go on an ice-fishing trip. If you're going to live like the Inuit, you'll have to get used to hunting your own food. Deep-frozen fish is a speciality but first you have to catch it. But forget a fishing line. You'll be using a spear so you might want to practice your aim before the trip. Cut a hole in the ice, using a traditional digging stick or a modern electric drill. Then dangle your lure (use something shiny like walrus tusk) into the hole. Then it's a case of waiting… If you're lucky, you'll nab a nice Arctic char. It tastes like salmon and is eaten raw. Save the fish bones for making sewing needles.

I HATE SHOPPING FOR NEW HATS!

4 Teach yourself Inuktitut. Then you'll be able to chat away to the Inuit in Alaska, Canada and Greenland. But beware. Inuktitut is horribly hard to speak and understand, and can take years and years to learn properly. Here's a list of useful phrases to get you started:

English	Inuktitut	How to say it
How are you?	Qanuipit?	Ka-nwee-peet
I am fine	Qunuinguttunga	Ka-nweeng-ut-toon-ga
I am hungry	Kaaktunga	Kak-toon-ga
I am cold	Qiuliqtunga	Ko-lick-toon-ga
I want to go fishing	Iqalliarumajunga	Ee-ka-lee-aa-roo-ma-jung-ga
I want to go by dogsled	Qimuksikkuuruma-vunga	Kim-mook-sick-koo-roo-mah-voon-ga
Help!	Ikajunga!	Ick-a-yung-ga
Goodbye!	Tavvauvusi!	Tah-vow-voo-see

5 Have a go at blanket tossing. It's a traditional Inuit sport but it's no ordinary blanket. It's made from walrus skins with a rope looped through holes around the edge. You jump on to the blanket, then the people standing around the outside grab hold of the rope. They pull on the blanket to toss you up and down, as much as 10 metres into the air. It's a bit like being on a walrus trampoline. Talk about landing on your feet. And if this isn't exciting enough for you, why not try … seal hopping (you balance on your knuckles and toes, then hop forward like a seal), or ear tug-of-war (you sit facing your opponent with a piece of string looped around each other's ears – right ear to right ear; left ear to left – and pull).

Five easy steps to becoming a musher*
(* That's what a dog sled driver's called.)

a) Pick your dogs. You'll need dogs that are tough, strong, and can cope with the cold. Siberian huskies or Alaskan Malamutes are ideal for the job. They can run for hours across the ice, pulling a heavy sled, and they've got super-thick coats to keep warm. Depending on the size of your sled, you'll need five to ten dogs so take along plenty of raw seal meat for them to munch on. Don't bother with a kennel. These marvellous mutts simply snuggle down in the snow at night.

b) Hitch the dogs to your sled. First, fit each dog with a specially padded harness that goes around its chest and is attached to the sled by a tugline. Then use a fan hitch or tandem hitch. In a fan hitch, the dogs fan out in front of the sled as they run. That way, if one dog crashes down a crevasse, the others don't follow behind. In a tandem hitch, pair the dogs up in a line. This works better for narrow trails.

c) Choose the best dog to lead. The lead dog will set the pace for the others in the pack and will also help to find the best track through the snow. Usually, the strongest and cleverest dog is chosen for this vital role. Behind it come the swing dogs who swing the team around bends in the trail. Then come the team dogs for power, and finally the wheel dogs, closest to the sled. They need to be calm and steady, and not get spooked by the sled moving.

SOME LEAD DOG!

d) Learn the right commands. Here are a few to start you off. Use a firm voice when you speak so the dogs know who's in charge.

- Hike! Hike! = Get moving/go faster
- Haw = Turn left
- Gee = Turn right
- Easy = Slow down
- On by = Go straight on
  Whoa! = Stop!

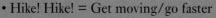

WHOA! STOP!

e) Get mushing! Congratulations! You're about to go for first drive. Mushing takes years of practice so don't worry about falling off. By the way, to stop in an emergency, push down on the brake bar at the back of the sled. 'Hike! Hike!'

WHOOOOOOOH!

Ask a South Pole scientist

Q 1: *So, what is a glaciologist?*

A: A glaciologist's a scientist who studies ice.

Q 2: *What does a glaciologist do?*

A: Glaciologists monitor ice sheets, sea ice, icebergs and glaciers with the help of high-tech equipment like radar and satellites. They try to find out how thick the ice is, if it's melting, if it's moving and things like that. They also take ice cores…

Q 3: *What's an, er, ice core?*

A: An ice core's a long stick of ice, like a giant, and I mean giant, ice lolly. Some of them are a whopping THREE KILOMETRES long. Glaciologists pull them out of deep holes they drill in the ice. By counting the layers in the core, they can tell how old the ice is. If a core's got 40,000 layers, the ice at the bottom's 40,000 years old! They can also tell what the weather was like way back by gawping at bubbles of gas in the ice.

Q 4: *Where do glaciologists work?*

A: A lot of a glaciologist's time is spent outside, visiting places with lots of ice. Antarctica's a brilliant place to work because there's so much of the shiny stuff about. To study sea ice, they also head to the Arctic.

Q 5: *Where do they live in Antarctica?*

A: They mostly live on research stations, called bases. They're like small towns, with living quarters, kitchens, hospitals, libraries, gyms and science labs. Some have even got luxury leisure facilities like cinemas and bowling alleys. But they also spend months on perishing field trips, camping in pyramid tents. That way, they can see the ice close up.

Q 6: *What do they eat on base?*

A: Any food has be transported thousands of kilometres by ship and plane. You can't just pop out to the shops. So it's mostly tinned, freeze-dried or frozen. Unless the scientists are lucky enough to be at the South Pole base where they grow their own veggies in a greenhouse. After weeks of this ghastly grub, it's no wonder the thought of a nice, fresh salad makes their mouths water. Freeze-dried cabbage, anyone?

Q 7: *How do you get about on the ice?*

A: It used to be by dog sled but huskies are now officially banned (see page 18). So snowmobiles and Sno Cats are used to carry people and pull sleds instead. Weather permitting, they also hitch lifts on small, specially designed aircraft. These polar planes are fitted with skis for landing on the ice.

Q 8: *Do they catch loads of colds?*

A: Er, not really. You don't actually get colds from being cold. Colds are spread by cold germs and Antarctica is so clean there aren't many germs around. In fact, they're sickeningly healthy and get regular check ups from the camp doctor. Aaatshoo!

EARTH—SHATTERING FACT

Scientists in Antarctica have found a brilliant way of studying the Southern Ocean, even when it's covered in ice. They glue little boxes containing electronic sensors to the heads of elephant seals. When the seals dive for food, the sensors pick up information about the water, like its temperature and saltiness. Apparently, it doesn't hurt the seals a bit, though I bet they feel rather seal-y, I mean, silly.

Can you speak beaker*?

* It's a kind of secret slang spoken by South Pole scientists (they're also called beakers). But what on Earth does it all mean?

I What is a snotsicle?
a) A sort of ice lolly
b) A snot icicle
c) A bicycle used at the Poles

2 What would you use a bog chisel for?
a) Cleaning the toilet
b) Mending your snowmobile
c) Testing the sea ice

3 When might you get greenout?
a) When you see green plants and trees
b) When you're on a ship and the sea gets choppy
c) When it's sprouts for tea again

4 What is degombling?
a) Brushing clumps of snow off your clothes
b) Combing clumps of hair off a musk ox
c) Talking nonsense because your lips are numb with frostbite

5 What is a dingle day like?
a) It's blowing a blizzard
b) It's fine and sunny
c) It's bucketing with rain

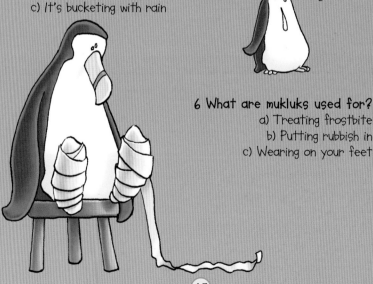

6 What are mukluks used for?
a) Treating frostbite
b) Putting rubbish in
c) Wearing on your feet

Answers:

1 b) A snotsicle's an icicle made from frozen snot dangling from the end of a person's nose. Snot very nice at all.

2 c) A bog chisel's an instrument with a wooden handle and a metal blade. It's used to probe sea ice to see if it's strong enough to walk on.

3 a) Greenout's the feeling of seeing and smelling greenery again after spending a long time on the ice.

4 a) Degombling's brushing clumps of snow off your clothes before you go inside. The clumps are known as gombles.

5 b) Dingle means good weather with good visibility for getting out and about.

6 c) Mukluks are really warm boots, based on a traditional Inuit pattern. The Inuit make them from sealskin and wear a pair of sealskin socks inside.

PARKY POLAR WILDLIFE

Imagine you're a wild animal looking for a place to call home, sweet home. You could pick somewhere warm and sunny, with the odd shower of refreshing rain. Sounds perfect. So why on Earth would you choose to live at the parky Poles where conditions are NOTHING LIKE THAT? Where you'll be faced with howling winds and freezing cold temperatures that'd make even the grittiest creature curl up and die. Where you'll be spending so much time staying warm and finding food, you won't have the energy to admire any views. Surprisingly, you won't be alone. Hundreds of horribly hardy animals and plucky plants already survive in this hostile habitat. Are you ready to find out about some spine-chilling survival strategies?

MAYBE WE SHOULD STOP FOR A BITE?

PERILOUS POLES FACT FILE

Name: POLAR BEAR
Where it lives: ON AND AROUND THE ARCTIC OCEAN
What it eats: SEALS, WALRUSES, BERRIES, SEAWEED

Long snout: For heating the freezing air before it hits the bear's lungs and for sniffing out seals. When a bear curls up in a ball to wait out a storm, it sometimes covers its conk with a furry paw to stop heat being lost.

Small head and ears: For cutting down on heat loss. The ears lie flat underwater.

Sharp teeth: For catching and chomping food. Polar bears tend to swallow their grub in chunks, rather than chewing it first.

Large paws: For walking over thin ice. Their size helps spread the bear's weight so it doesn't fall in. (On very thin ice, bears crawl on their bellies to spread their weight out even more.) They're also furry for gripping the ice.

Webbed front paws: For swimming. The bear uses its front paws for paddling and its back paws for steering.

Thick, fur coat: For keeping out the cold. There are two layers of fur so the bear stays warm even in temperatures of −45°C. In fact, their fur's so superbly snug, bears regularly overheat. The fur's also oily to keep bears waterproof.

White colour: For hiding the bear when it's hunting seals on the ice. Strictly speaking, the fur isn't actually white. It only looks it because the hairs are hollow (to trap warm air) and scatter light.

Thick blubber: For extra warmth. It's a layer of fat up to 12 centimetres thick under the bear's skin. It also helps the bear to float in the water.

Sharp claws: They're curved and more than 5 centimetres long and cunningly designed for swiping at seals and gripping the ice.

Bumpy soles: Tiny bumps on the soles of the bear's feet help it keep a grip on the ice.

Polar bear facts:

• Polar bears are enormous. They can stand around 2.5 metres tall and weigh a whopping 600 kilograms. Not surprisingly, this makes them the biggest meat-eaters on land.

• Polar bears love to go swimming, even though the water's fr-fr-freezing. They can swim a staggering 100 kilometres without a rest, using a sort of doggy paddle.

• A polar bear's favourite meal is seal and they're especially fond of ringed seals. But they'll also hunt and kill humans if they're very, very hungry.

• Polar bears have such sharp noses, they can sniff out a seal even when it's UNDER THE ICE. Then they wait for it to come up for air … and pounce.

BE POLAR BEAR AWARE

Five tips for avoiding a polar bear attack:

Stay on the look-out. Polar bears are horribly unpredictable and horribly hard to outwit. Your best bet for staying alive is spotting the bear, and getting outta there, before the bear spots you.

Keep away from cubs. Woe betide you if a mother polar bear thinks you're cooing over her cubs. Before you've had chance to take a snap, she'll have your head inside her jaws.

Listen out for warning sounds. These include growling, hissing, snorting and roaring. If the bear puts its head down and ears back, it's about to charge.

Take a friend along. You'll less likely to be a target if you're part of a group. Make yourself look even bigger by holding your coat above your head.

Stand your ground. If a bear charges, don't run away. The bear's plenty fast enough to outrun you. If you can, move to a safe shelter, ever so slowly.

HORRIBLE HEALTH WARNING

Polar bears might look cute and cuddly but they can also be deadly killers, especially if they're hungry. As a man in Churchill, Canada, found out to his cost. In 1983, the man was rummaging around in the ruins of a recently burned-down hotel. He found some meat in the freezer and began stuffing it into his pockets ... just in time to be pounced on by a peckish polar bear who reckoned it was time for lunch.

PERILOUS POLES FACT FILE

Name: EMPEROR PENGUIN
Where it lives: ANTARCTICA
What it eats: FISH, SQUID

Perilous polar facts:
• It's the biggest of all the penguins (and one of the biggest sea birds), standing more than 1 metre tall and weighing around 40 kilograms.

• It's one of four kinds of penguin that live on icy Antarctica. (The others are the Adelie, the gentoo and the chinstrap.) But it lives in enormous colonies up to 40,000 birds strong so it never feels lonely.

• It has got wings but it can't fly. Instead, it's a superb swimmer, using its wings as flippers to speed through the sea. It steers with its feet and tail.

• It's the only animal that breeds on the ice IN THE MIDDLE OF WINTER when the temperature's as low as –45°C and it's blowing a gale.

Cool polar creature competition

Which of these two creatures is the coolest at keeping warm?

PENGUINS

HUMANS

① FEATHERS v CLOTHES

THICK OVERLAPPING FEATHERS

WATERPROOF AND WARM UNDERNEATH

LAYERS OF WARM, WATERPROOF CLOTHES

② BLUBBER v FAT

EXTRA-THICK LAYER OF FAT UNDER THE SKIN FOR WARMTH

THINNISH LAYER OF FAT UNDER SKIN

③ BODY SHAPE v BODY SHAPE

ROUNDED BODY SHAPE TO REDUCE HEAT LOSS

LONG, GANGLY BODY SHAPE

④ FEET AND WINGS v ARMS AND LEGS

SMALL FEET AND WINGS TO REDUCE HEAT LOSS

LONG ARMS AND LONG LEGS

⑤ BLOOD CIRCULATION

SPECIAL BLOOD CIRCULATION SYSTEMS SO THEIR FEET DON'T FREEZE ON THE ICE

TWO PAIRS OF THICK SOCKS TO STOP FROSTBITTEN TOES

⑥ BEHAVIOUR

HUDDLE TOGETHER FOR WARMTH

LIVE IN HOUSE AND HUDDLE ROUND FIRES

⑦ TOENAILS

STRONG TOENAILS FOR GRIPPING THE ICE

OVERGROWN TOENAILS THAT NEED CLIPPING

⑧ BEAK v NOSE

COVERED IN FEATHERS TO KEEP WARMTH IN

NOT COVERED SO AT RISK OF GETTING FROSTBITTEN

And the winner is… Well, the penguins, of course, by a million miles. They're brilliantly designed for their icy lives. Whereas, a human's probably better off staying at home.

75

Polar animal survival guide

Wear a warm fur coat. The Arctic fox's summer coat is thin and grey to match the rocks. But in winter, it changes into a thick, woolly, white fur coat. Not only is it wonderfully warm, it's also brilliant at blending in with the icy background. What's more, the fox's feet are so fabulously furry it can walk across the ice without getting frostbite.

Survival rating: *****

Get a very thick skin. Walruses keep warm in the Arctic with a thick layer of blubber (fat) beneath their skin. Their blubber's up to 15 centimetres thick (that's a pile of 15 books like this) and can take up a third of the walrus's body weight. The ingenious Inuit use chunks of walrus blubber for catching, er, walruses.

Survival rating: ****

Stock up on antifreeze. For fish living in the polar seas, freezing to death's a real risk. But amazingly, that doesn't bother ice fish in Antarctica. They've got a type of chemical in their blood that stops them freezing. On land, tiny creatures like mites and springtails also use this horribly successful strategy.

Survival rating: *****

Grow as big as possible. Some enormous sea creatures grow in Antarctica, even though they're pretty paltry elsewhere. Take giant worms bigger than your thumbs, and seriously scary sea spiders a thousand times normal size. The reason they're so outsized is because it takes them much longer to burn off their food in the cold.

Survival rating: ***

Keep your eyes open. Hardy Weddell seals live under the Antarctic ice where they feed on deep-sea fish and squid. Luckily, they're daring divers and can hold their breath for an hour while they hunt for prey. They've also got extra-large eyes for seeing in the gloomy water.
Survival rating: ✳✳✳

> I HOPE THERE'S SOMETHING FISHY GOING ON HERE!

HORRIBLE HEALTH WARNING

By the way, if you happen to be a Weddell seal, make sure you look after your teeth. You'll need them to gnaw holes in the ice so you can keep coming up for air. Otherwise, you won't be able to breathe. Eventually, your teeth will wear out so it'll be curtains anyway.

Odd polar plant out

Which of these perky plants *doesn't* bloom at the Poles?
a) Willow
b) Hairgrass
c) Ice plant
d) Rock tripe
e) Snow algae

Answers:

The only plant you *won't* find at the Poles is **c)**. All of the others have special deep-freeze features that help them bloom happily in the bitter cold.

a) There aren't any trees in Antarctica (it's just too bloomin' cold) but titchy willow, birch and alder trees sprout in the Arctic. But they're so small you could step right over the top of them. And the reason they keep their heads down is to stay out of the howling wind. By the way, if you've got toothache, try chewing on an Arctic willow twig. That's what the locals do.

b) Only two kinds of flowers bloom in icy Antarctica – the hardy hairgrass and the plucky pearlwort. The hairgrass looks like, er, grass, and the pearlwort's a sort of carnation. Handily, they both manage to keep growing even when it's frosty and freezing cold.

c) Despite its frosty-sounding name, the ice plant doesn't grow on the ice. It doesn't even come close. It actually comes from the desperate deserts of Africa but it's also a popular plant for people to grow on rockeries in their back gardens.

d) Rock tripe's a kind of lichen, a horribly hardy polar plant. Lichens are ideally suited for polar living because they love blooming on bare rocks, with only the odd bit of seal or penguin poo for nourishment. Rock tripe's found in the Arctic where it was munched by peckish polar explorers when they'd run out of food.

e) Snow algae are tiny plants that turn large patches of polar ice a pretty shade of pink or red. But this dazzling display's not simply for show. The plants' red colouring works a bit like suncream and stops them getting frazzled in the powerful polar sun.

POLES
IN
PERIL

Still can't make up your mind about whether to set off for the perilous Poles. Or stay at home and veg out in front of the telly? Still worried you won't come back alive from the icy wastes? Well, you'd better get your skates on if you're thinking of visiting. Leave it much longer and there might not be any bloomin' ice left for you to investigate. What's happening is this. The Earth's climate is getting warmer and scientists are noticing the Poles are starting to melt at an alarming rate. Yep, the Poles are in serious peril and most geographers agree horrible humans have only themselves to blame.

PERILOUS POLES FACT FILE

Name: GLOBAL WARMING

What is it: THE WAY THE EARTH'S TEMPERATURE IS WARMING UP

How does it happen:

a) GREENHOUSE GASES FROM THE ATMOSPHERE TRAP HEAT COMING FROM THE SUN.

b) THESE GASES COME FROM FACTORIES, VEHICLES AND BURNING DOWN RAINFORESTS.

c) THIS IS CAUSING THE EARTH TO WARM UP ... AT AN ALARMING RATE.

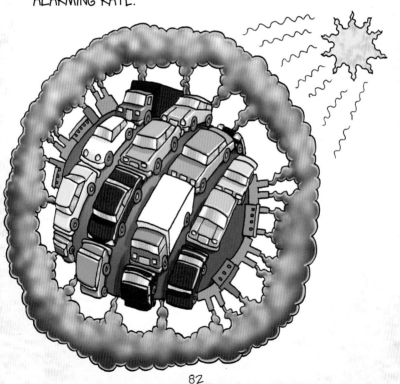

Perilous polar facts:

• Some global warming is a good thing. Otherwise, the Earth would be too chilly for anything to live on. Trouble is, the amount of greenhouse gases is growing too fast, largely because of things horrible humans are doing.

• The Poles are warming up faster than anywhere else on the planet. And it's having a devastating effect. Sea ice and ice caps are melting, and glaciers are shrinking fast.

• In 2007, satellites noticed the normally ice-infested Northwest Passage was clear. For the first time in history, ships could sail right along its length.

• Even more worryingly, in 2008, so much ice had melted in the Arctic Ocean, it was possible to sail right around the North Pole for the very first time.

Melting moments: the aftermath
If the ice melts, it'll mean catastrophic consequences for…

The place…
Scientists reckon the Arctic sea ice is melting so fast, it could be gone in summer by the year 2013. And the Greenland ice cap's starting to look horribly thin. If this colossal ice cube melted, it would send sea levels soaring, flooding coastal cities and low-lying islands. Besides, in Arctic Alaska and Siberia, the permafrost (year-round frozen ground) is thawing for the first time in thousands of years. Buildings and roads can't stand up on the soggy slush and slump into the ground.

The wildlife…
Polar bears rely on the sea ice to go hunting. They need to fatten up on seal fat in summer to last them through winter when food is scarce. But, with the ice melting earlier each year, they're facing a horribly bleak future. Meanwhile, the Southern Ocean's also warming up so cold-water creatures can't

THIS IS FLIPPING AWKWARD!

84

function properly. Take lopsided limpets, for starters. In warm water, they can't flip themselves shell-side up if they land the wrong way round. And that's vital for avoiding icebergs that scrape along the sea bed.

The climate...

Apart from soaring sea levels, the loss of the perishing polar ice could spell disaster for the world's climate. The ice acts like an colossal air-conditioning system, reflecting awesome amounts of sunlight back into space. On top of this, the seas around the Poles soak up heat and spread it around the world in gigantic currents. This keeps our planet cool enough for humans, and other animals, to live on. Otherwise, we'd all be toast.

The people...

The Inuit have hunted animals on the sea ice for centuries. But things are changing fast. With the sea freezing later and melting earlier, they're having trouble finding enough food. Along the coast, they also rely on the sea ice to protect their villages from the wind and waves. Now, their homes are at risk of being lashed by some serious storms that are set to get even wilder…

A village on the edge

Shishmaref, northern Alaska, 2009

The village of Shishmaref stands on a tiny island off the north–west coast of Alaska in the icy Chukchi Sea. For more than 400 years, it has been home to hundreds of local Inuit people. But now, because of global warming, the ground beneath the villagers' feet is literally being swallowed up by the sea.

What's happening is the permafrost their houses are built on is thawing at an alarming rate, and the ground's crumbling away like sand. Several houses have already slumped into the sea, and many more are starting to slip.

To make matters worse, the sea ice around the island is melting as the temperature rises. For centuries, this essential ice has locked up the sea around the island, protecting the land from being battered by the wind and waves. Not any longer. Today, serious storms lash the seashore, eating away at the already crumbling cliffs, despite the villagers' desperate attempts to hold the waves back with sandbags and barricades. And the storms are getting stronger and more frequent.

For generations, the villagers have lived a traditional way of life, hunting seals, walruses and polar bears for their food and clothing. Now they've made an agonizing decision. If they stay put, their lives are likely to be in great danger. So, they've all voted to leave the island and settle in a new village on the mainland.

HORRIBLE HEALTH WARNING

If you're popping across to Antarctica, leave your budgie at home. Astonishingly, pets like budgies, goldfish and even dogs and cats have been found on some of the bases. Trouble is, they carry diseases that spread to the local seals and penguins, making them seriously sick. And that's not all. Penguins have also been pole-axed by diseases spread by the leftovers of the scientists' roast-chicken dinners.

EPILOGUE

Congratulations! You've braved some of the harshest conditions on the planet and your frostbitten fingers are thawing out nicely. You've battled with blizzards, dodged crevasses, and you've come back in one piece. But before you start boring everyone silly with your holiday snaps, spare a thought for the future of the perilous Poles. Is it really all doom and gloom? Well, it all depends on your point of view...

Actually, global warming's good news. For starters, there's oodles of precious oil and minerals like diamonds under the Arctic ice – where it's horribly hard to get at. But with the ice melting, people won't have to dig so deep. And that's not all. The warmer weather means farmers in Greenland are able to grow crops, like broccoli, for the first time. Great news if you like eating your greens.

Global warming's already a disaster for polar people and wildlife. As the ice melts, the Inuit's traditional lifestyle is vanishing fast, and animals, like polar bears, are starving. The Poles are vitally important – even if you never get to go there yourself. They're such amazing wildernesses, they're unique places to study. Trouble is, it may already be too late.

Of course, the best way to make your mind up is to see the perilous Poles for yourself. What's that? You've only just got back from your last trip and you haven't even had time to unpack? Never mind about that. Hitch a lift on one of the latest scientific expeditions that are heading off to check up on the Poles. An expedition like the one led by British explorer, Pen Hadow, in 2009 to measure the thickness of the melting Arctic sea ice. That way, you'll get to use your new-found survival skills *and* help protect the Poles at the same time. Now, how cool is that?

Perilous polar websites

If you're interested in finding out more about the perilous Poles, here are some websites to check out:

www.discoveringantarctica.org.uk
Activities, pictures, video clips and fact sheets to help you find out more about awesome Antarctica.

www.antarctica.ac.uk
Find out all about the British Antarctic Survey and read the gripping diaries of some real-life polar scientists.

www.antarcticconnection.com
Everything you ever wanted to know about Antarctic weather - guaranteed to send shivers down your spine.

http://nsidc.org
The website of the National Snow and Ice Data Center in the USA with loads of brilliant facts about, er, snow and ice.

www.spri.cam.ac.uk
The Scott Polar Institute website with facts about the Arctic, its people, landscape and wildlife.

www.weio.org
All about the events in the World Eskimo-Indian Olympics and how you can take part.

http://pbsg.npolar.no/en/index.html
The Polar Bear Specialist Group website, packed with information and articles about the world's polar bears.

INDEX

Get your teeth into more
Horrible Geography
Handbooks!

**WILD ANIMALS,
WICKED WEATHER,
VILE VOLCANOES &
PLANET IN PERIL**
are in the shops
NOW!